►HOME **LIGHTING** IDEAS◄

ENTRANCES AND LIVING ROOMS

First published in the United States of America by:
Rockport Publishers, Inc.
146 Granite Street
Rockport, Massachusetts 01966-1299
Telephone: (508) 546-9590
Fax: (508) 546-7141

Distributed to the book trade and art trade
in the United States by:
Rockport Publishers
Rockport, Massachusetts 01966-1299

ISBN 1-56496-288-1

10 9 8 7 6 5 4 3 2 1

ART DIRECTOR
Lynne Havighurst

DESIGNER
Sara Day Graphic Design

FRONT COVER PHOTOGRAPH
Lighting Designer: Denton Knapp, Interior Designers: Charles Falls and Kenton Knapp, Photographer: Patrick Barta

BACK COVER CREDITS
Appear on pages 27, 29, and 30.

Photo on page 1 also appears on page 27. Photo on page 4 also appears on page 18. Photo on page 5 also appears on page 17. Photo on page 20 also appears on page 28. Photo on page 21 also appears on page 30. Photo on page 42- Lighting and Interior Designer: Claudia Librett, Photographer: Durston Saylor. Photo on page 43-Lighting Designer: Linda Ferry, Interior Designers: Tony Carrasco and Greg Warner, Photographer: Russell Abraham. Photo on page 44-Lighting and Interior Designers: Charles H. Grebmeier and Gunnar Burkland, Photographer: Eric Zepeda. Photo on page 45-Lighting and Interior Designer: Ruth Soforenko, Photographer: Ron Starr. Photo on page 48-Lighting Designer: Pam Morris, Interior Designers: Neal and Bonnie Singer, Photographer: Dennis Anderson.

Printed by Welpac, Singapore.

HOME **LIGHTING** IDEAS

ENTRANCES AND LIVING ROOMS

Randall Whitehead

ROCKPORT
PUBLISHERS

Rockport Publishers
Rockport, Massachusetts

Entrances:
Setting the tone

The entry to a house establishes the mood and tone for the rest of the home. In the entrance, lighting can be used to open up space and provide a hospitable environment for the welcomed visitor. Through the use of proper lighting design, a dark and cramped entryway can appear spacious and become a warm and comforting area for guests.

The two most common goals of lighting design are to make a small entry appear larger, or to make a large entry feel more intimate. Creative lighting can help to transform this important space. Well-designed lighting can both show off architec-

tural detail and hide flaws.

The entry is normally a pass-through area and a greeting area for guests; people don't usually spend much time there. This leaves just a moment for the home-owner to make a statement about the mood of the activity to come.

Changing the Mood

As a rule, the brighter the space, the more animated the event. A dimly-lit room provides a relaxed, intimate atmosphere for its occupants.

To make people feel more comfortable in an entry with a very high ceiling, install translucent wall sconces. This will create a secondary ceiling line that gives the desired human scale and makes the space feel less intimidating. Reflecting light from the ceiling will help make low ceilings seem higher and small entries seem larger.

Ambient illumination should fill the space surrounding the entry with welcoming light. Fill light is especially important in this area. The gentle glow of illumination will help people feel at ease in new surroundings and flatter both homeowners and guests. Good ambient light in the entry can transform what is sometimes an awkward moment into a more comfortable and enjoyable encounter.

Entry lighting can also energize a person's impression of a home: highlighting a dramatic painting, sculpture, or architectural detail draws attention to objects of interest, and will simultaneously welcome and impress visitors.

Illusion

Not all lighting solutions directly involve the use of luminaires. Mirrors, for example, can be used to create the illusion of greater space or light. Lining one wall with mirrors can make a room seem to expand in size. Strategically placed mirrors will also keep wall areas located farthest from the windows from falling into darkness or seeming less important. Entries come in all shapes and sizes. Lighting can help you redefine this envelope of space.

Do you want the entrance to appear larger or more intimate? Do you want to create a look that dazzles, or produce a sense of homey comfort? How about a combination of both? It is possible. For example, in a cramped entry area you can use illusion and lighting to "steal" part of another room and visually incorporate it into the entry area. In addition to using mirrors, you might also consider employing such techniques as using glass block to divide space, or directing an accent light onto an object in an adjacent room to make that area seem like part of the entrance.

Stairways in an entry area provide additional opportunities for visual expansiveness. Illuminated, stairs make a room seem larger and provide another focus for the guest's

attention upon entering the home. Lighting a painting mounted on the wall along the stairway, or illuminating plants or a sculpture on a stair landing, can also help a small entry assume the appearance of a grand entrance hall. Switching and dimming systems can take the same entry that was made to look dramatic for a big party or event and instantly transform it into an intimate greeting area for small gatherings: lighting can and should be that flexible. By using an integrated dimming system, homeowners can create whatever kind of setting and tone they would like. Lighting can be used to set the mood and even provide timing cues for the evening's activities.

Minimizing Focal Points

Instead of filling up an entry area with lots of objects, keep the decor simple and spotlight a few specific details. This places greater visual value on those pieces. There often is only enough time to enjoy a few items in the entry before moving on to the next space. Fill light helps homeowners and their guests look their best. Recessed downlights by

themselves make people look tired and makes a space feel smaller than it actually is. Think of the entrance as a preview to the main event of your home. It is a taste of things to come.

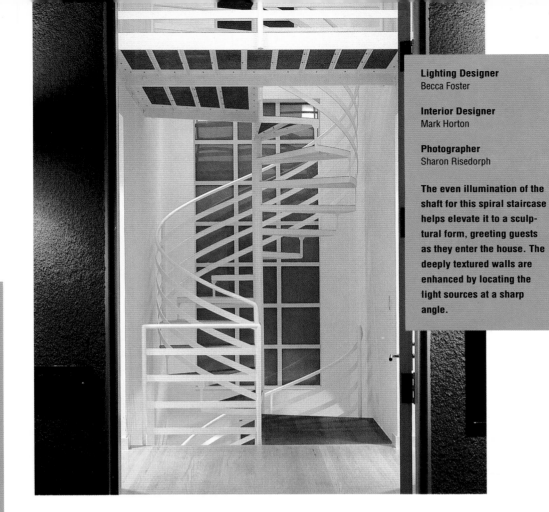

Lighting Designer
Becca Foster

Interior Designer
Mark Horton

Photographer
Sharon Risedorph

The even illumination of the shaft for this spiral staircase helps elevate it to a sculptural form, greeting guests as they enter the house. The deeply textured walls are enhanced by locating the light sources at a sharp angle.

Lighting Designer
Catherine Ng and
Randall Whitehead

Interior Designer
Lawrence Masnada

Architect
Sid Del Mar Leach

Photographer
Kenneth Rice

The almost surreal look of this illuminated railing is accomplished by using fiber optics mounted inside a channel routed into the underside of the Lucite. The owner can transform the color and feel of the entire railing simply by turning a color wheel located within the remote light source.

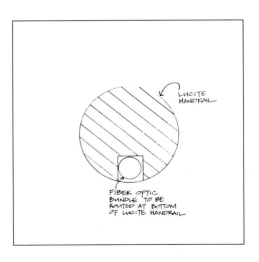

LUCITE HANDRAIL

FIBER OPTIC BUNDLE TO BE ROUTED AT BOTTOM OF LUCITE HANDRAIL

Lighting Designer
Claudia Librett

Interior Designer
Claudia Librett

Photographer
Durston Saylor

A combination of recessed fixtures and intra-beam uplighting helps add drama to this massive space.

Lighting Designer
Randall Whitehead and
Bart Smyth

Photographer
Randall Whitehead

**Incandescent mini-strip
light fixtures under the
nosing of these stairs add
architectural interest,
especially at dusk when the
evening sky turns a blue-
lavender color and floods in
through the central skylight.**

Lighting Designer
Randall Whitehead

Interior Designer
Marlene Grant

Photographer
Russell Abraham

**This ziggurat corner detail
hides rose-colored compact
fluorescent bulbs.**

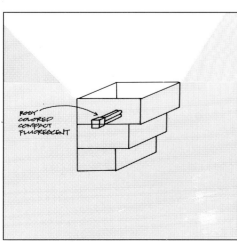

ROSY
COLORED
COMPACT
FLUORESCENT

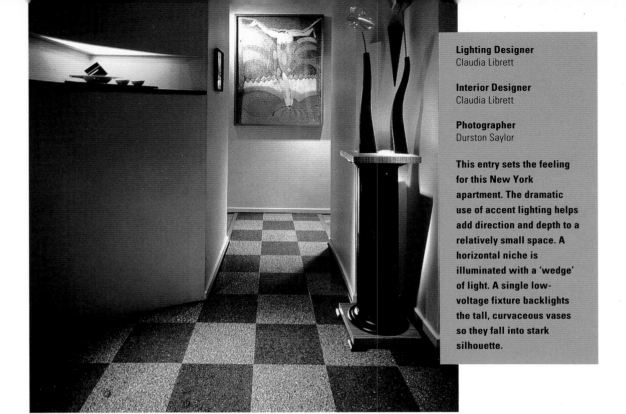

Lighting Designer
Claudia Librett

Interior Designer
Claudia Librett

Photographer
Durston Saylor

This entry sets the feeling for this New York apartment. The dramatic use of accent lighting helps add direction and depth to a relatively small space. A horizontal niche is illuminated with a 'wedge' of light. A single low-voltage fixture backlights the tall, curvaceous vases so they fall into stark silhouette.

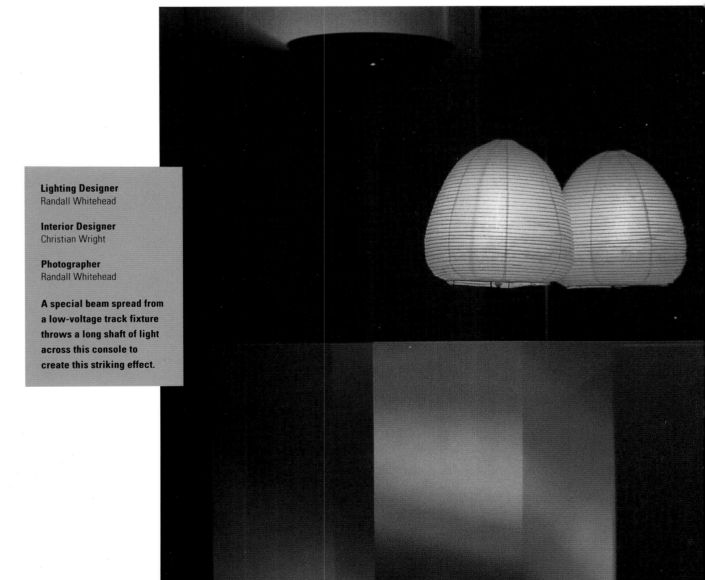

Lighting Designer
Randall Whitehead

Interior Designer
Christian Wright

Photographer
Randall Whitehead

A special beam spread from a low-voltage track fixture throws a long shaft of light across this console to create this striking effect.

Lighting Designer
Charles J. Grebmeier
and Gunnar Burklund

Interior Designer
Charles J. Grebmeier
and Gunnar Burklund

Photographer
Eric Zepeda

**Day and night shots show
how light can affect a
space.**

Lighting Designer
Randall Whitehead
and Catherine Ng

Interior Designer
Christian Wright and
Gerald Simpkins

Photographer
Ben Janken

The 3-foot-wide hall was made to seem visually large by mirroring between three shallow columns. The original candlestick-type wall brackets were removed and wall sconces, mimicking the ziggurat details of the architecture, became "winged capitols." Several recessed adjustable fixtures light the hallway and art, while the glass block is illuminated by fill light in the kitchen beyond.

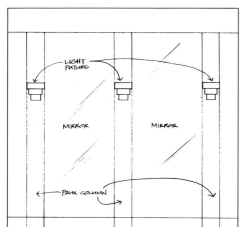

Lighting Designer
Randall Whitehead

Interior Designer
Christian Wright and
Gerald Simpkins

Photographer
Randall Whitehead

A 20-watt halogen track fixture brings out the form and colors of this sculptural flower arrangement.

Lighting Designer
Kenton Knapp and
Robert Truax

Interior Designer
Charles Falls

Photographer
Mary Nichols

Recessed adjustable
fixtures breathe life into the
art as metal wall sconces
show off the ceiling
details.

Lighting Designer
Kenton Knapp and
Robert Truax

Interior Designer
Charles Falls and
Kenton Knapp

Photographer
Eric Zepeda

Lowered fixtures emphasize
the relief of gilded carvings
and the coloration of the ori-
ental screen, as a torchlike
wall sconce fills the area
with a pleasing illumination.

Lighting Designer
Becca Foster

Interior Designer
Joseph Michalsky

Photographer
Philip Pavliger

This detail shot of the entry
shows how dramatic and
special a space can
become with the use of
well-placed lighting. A pair
of downlights brings out the
color and texture of the
weaving and the spectacular
flower arrangement.

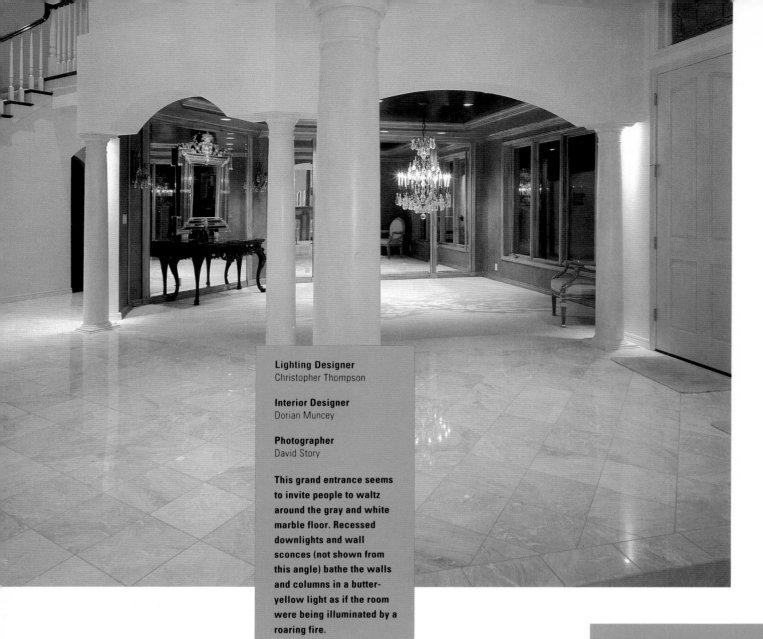

Lighting Designer
Christopher Thompson

Interior Designer
Dorian Muncey

Photographer
David Story

This grand entrance seems to invite people to waltz around the gray and white marble floor. Recessed downlights and wall sconces (not shown from this angle) bathe the walls and columns in a butter-yellow light as if the room were being illuminated by a roaring fire.

Lighting Designer
Christopher Thompson

Interior Designer
Dorian Muncey

Photographer
David Story

The incredible ceiling height of this entry is brought down to a more human scale with the addition of a grand chandelier. The room's real illumination comes from the recessed downlights and wall sconces so that the chandelier can be dimmed to a soft sparkle.

Lighting Designer
Nan Rosenblatt

Interior Designer
Nan Rosenblatt

Photographer
Russell Abraham

Two recessed adjustable fixtures highlight a floral painting while incandescent mini strip light fixtures, hidden behind the perimeter, illuminate the domed ceiling detail.

Lighting Designer
Kenton Knapp and
Robert Truax

Interior Designer
Charles Falls

Photographer
Mary Nichols

Well-placed lighting helps
the exterior become part of
the interior space.

Lighting Designer
Randall Whitehead

Interior Designer
Lawrence Masnada

Photographer
John Benson

The dark-colored surfaces of
the entry recede into the
background allowing the
large tropical arrangement to
take prominence. The
recessed adjustable fixtures
provide the accent light for
the flowers and pick up the
white floor tiles.

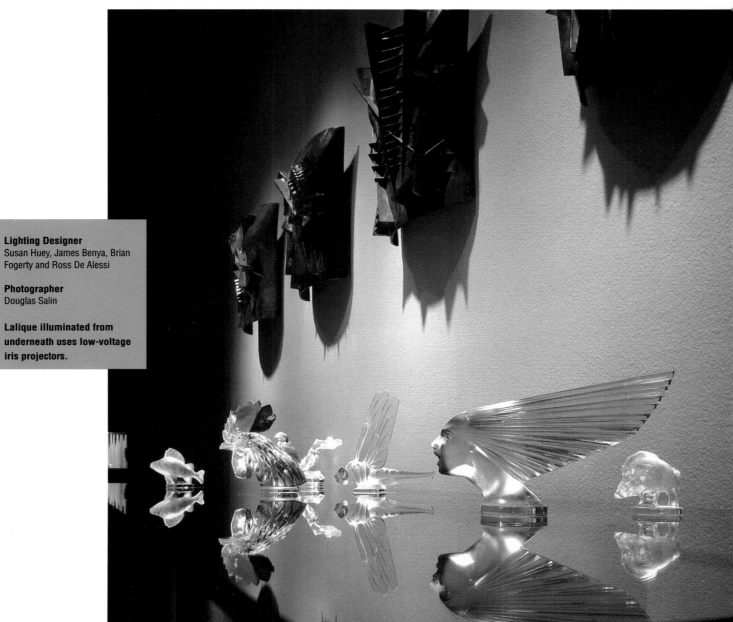

Lighting Designer
Susan Huey, James Benya, Brian
Fogerty and Ross De Alessi

Photographer
Douglas Salin

Lalique illuminated from
underneath uses low-voltage
iris projectors.

Lighting Designer
Kenton Knapp and
Robert Truax

Interior Designer
Charles Falls

Photographer
Mary Nichols

Recessed adjustable fixtures using low-voltage lamps emphasize the urns and screen.

Lighting Designer
Kenton Knapp and
Robert Truax

Interior Designer
Charles Falls and Kenton Knapp

Photographer
Eric Zepeda

Illuminated shelving gives great impact to this collection of art objects.

Lighting Designer
Kenton Knapp

Interior Designer
Charles Falls and
Kenton Knapp

Photographer
Patrick Barta

These totem poles greet visitors as they enter this striking Lake Tahoe residence.

Living Rooms:
Layering Comfort with Drama

The living room should be a soft island of illumination that invites people to relax and converse. Layering light creates an environment that is humanizing and dramatic at the same time. Wall sconces and torchieres can generally provide the ambient illumination, which softens shadows on people's faces. Recessed adjustable fixtures or track lighting can be used to add the necessary accent light.

Since the living room is the most public room in the home it should also be the most dazzling, *and* it should have the most flexible lighting design. There will be occasions that call for the room to look bright and warm, as if a roaring fire were filling it with soft illumination. People are naturally drawn to light; they tend to congregate where there is the greatest amount of illumination. Other occasions call for a more intimate atmosphere: dim the ambient lights and brighten the accent lights to help make a large space more cozy.

The Way It Was

The living room was once a formal area used only for company. There was a certain coldness about living rooms, an austerity that kept everybody out. Much of this had to do with the lighting itself. In traditional living room designs, two table lamps flank a sofa while an additional lamp is placed on top of a chest, or a floor lamp is placed next to a chair. When the lamps are turned on, their linen shades visually overpower the room, causing everything else to fall into secondary focus. They also create glare, which makes the space feel uncomfortable.

Layering with Light

With the introduction of layering light, in which specific fixtures perform specific functions, decorative fixtures such as table lamps and chandeliers can be dimmed to emit a glow of light without dominating the space.

Ambient Light

The first priority when layering light is to create adequate ambient light. Most typical rooms have a ceiling height of eight feet, which poses some problems. One solution would be to install four wall sconces, mounted two feet from the ceiling and equipped with 150-watt (or less) lamps, and a dimmer switch. This arrangement will give the room a warm glow. A possible alternative would be to use a pair of torchieres flanking either the fireplace or a piece of art, although the illumination would be less even than with four wall sconces. If the room is large, try using two torchieres placed diagonally from each other.

Torchieres provide excellent ambient light: filling the volume of space with an overall illumination that softens the shadows on people's faces and highlights architectural details. If you have a white or light-colored ceiling, the torchiere can provide a suitable secondary task light for reading newspapers and magazines. For serious reading, a pharmacy-type lamp, that positions the light between your head and the work surface, is recommended.

Living rooms with nine-foot or higher ceilings offer more open options. For example, pendant luminaires or cove lighting (light source hidden behind a crown molding or valence) would work equally well. Living rooms with gabled ceilings and support beams that are parallel to the floor offer an additional option. In this situation, linear strip lighting can be mounted on top of the beams to provide ambient light from a hidden source.

Accent Lights

Once you have decided how to give the living room ambient light, the next step is to make a decision about accent lighting. The type of luminaire you choose for the source of accent lighting should be flexible, to accommodate new arrangements of furniture and art. Remember, straight downlights used for accent lighting offer no flexibility whatsoever: if the highlighted object is moved, you will be left with a circle of light on the floor. Recessed, adjustable luminaires are more adaptable, and come in both line-voltage and low-voltage versions. The low-voltage version has the additional advantage of small size, which draws less attention to the unit itself.

If your home already has recessed luminaires, you can keep the housings (the main part of a recessed luminaire installed inside the ceiling) and replace the trims (the visible part of a recessed unit, attached to the housing) with line- or low-voltage adjustable versions. In new construction and remodel projects, successful accent lighting depends on what is to be highlighted, so add accent lights after drawing the furniture plan.

Task Lighting

The last consideration in the layout of the lighting design is task lighting. The main function of task lighting in the living room is for reading or related activities. Since the best position for a reading light is between one's head and where one's attention is focused, a pharmacy-type luminaire or a tabletop luminaire works best. If the floor plan has furniture in the middle of the room, it's a good idea to specify floor plugs so that cords don't cross the floor to a wall outlet. Crawl space or basement accessibility is a necessity in a remodel project.

Remember, the combination of all the elements of lighting—task, ambient, and accent—must be considered in order to create a totally functional and adaptable lighting design.

Lighting Designer
Claudia Librett

Interior Designer
Claudia Librett

Photographer
Durston Saylor

The interaction of light and shadow add a great deal of interest to this living space. The low-voltage PAR36 fixtures highlight various objects while the wall sconces provide the necessary ambient light.

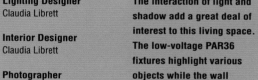

Lighting Designer
Ross De Alessi and Brian Fogerty

Interior Designer
George Saxe and Ted Cohen

Photographer
Ross De Alessi

Art turns this living room into an enchanted gallery.

Lighting Designer
Linda Ferry

Interior Designer
Michelle Pheasant

Photographer
Gil Edelstein

A flexible light plan accommodates the functions of each room and still gives a unified sense to the interior.

Lighting Designer
Donald Maxcy

Interior Designer
William Reno

Photographer
Russell Abraham

A display case becomes
the focal point in this
room with the use of well-
concealed incandescent
mini-strip lights. Multiple
recessed adjustable fix-
tures bring other objects
into focus.

Lighting Designer
Linda Esselstein

Interior Designer
Sharon Marston

Photographer
Russell Abraham

A simple low-voltage sys-
tem adds dramatic
emphasis to this living
room. The marble fire-
place is almost art in
itself while the two bisque
urns stand guard.

Lighting Designer
Randall Whitehead

Interior Designer
Lawrence Masnada

Photographer
Cecile Keefe

The lighting, when dimmed
to a low level, bathes this
San Francisco living room in
a radiant glow of amber
light. The walls are washed
with illumination coming
from behind a valance detail
that surrounds the entire
room.

Lighting Designer
Linda Ferry

Interior Designer
David Allen Smith

Photographer
Douglas Salin

A low-voltage wire system acts as both sculpture and a source of accent lighting while the halogen pendant fixture adds fill light to the space and highlights the bowl of fruit on the table.

Lighting Designer
Linda Ferry

Interior Designer
John Schneider

Photographer
Gil Edelstein

In this study, two concrete wall sconces add a soft background light to balance out the room with the addition of accents on the bookcases using recessed wall washers.

Lighting Designer
Ruth Soforenko

Interior Designer
Ruth Soforenko

Photographer
Russell Abraham

Track fixtures add dramatic highlights to this living room.

Lighting Designer
James Benya

Interior Designer
Sharon Marston

Photographer
John Vaughan

This dynamic living room is
intriguing and exciting at the
same time. The brass and
black torchieres provide a
calming ambient light while
low-voltage fixtures highlight the table and screens.
Light passing through the
plant branches projects
shadows onto the adjoining
wall.

Lighting Designer
Randall Whitehead

Interior Designer
Christian Wright and
Gerald Simpkins

Photographer
Randall Whitehead

A blue filter enhances the
color of this vase.

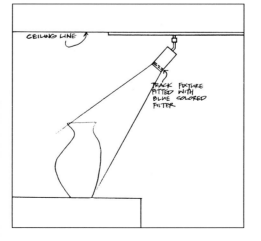

CEILING LINE

TRACK FIXTURE
FITTED WITH
BLUE COLORED
FILTER

Lighting Designer
Kenton Knapp and Robert Truax

Interior Designer
Charles Falls

Photographer
Eric Zepeda

**Each shelf is individually
illuminated to create this
stunning space.**

Lighting Designer
Donald Maxcy

Interior Designer
Donald Maxcy

Photographer
Russell Abraham

This room has tremendous texture and dimension through the use of concealed recessed adjustable fixtures and custom-designed, fan-shaped wall sconces.

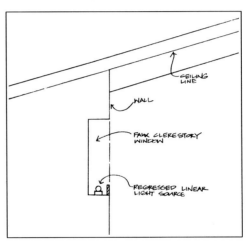

Lighting Designer
Randall Whitehead
and Catherine Ng

Interior Designer
Linda Bradshaw-Allen

Photographer
Ben Janken

The wall sconces, when dimmed, change from a bright white light to a warm amber glow. The linear incandescent sources inset into the faux clerestory windows set off these subtle architectural details.

Lighting Designer
Catherine Ng and
Randall Whitehead

Interior Designer
Lawrence Masnada

Photographer
Kenneth Rice

This thrilling space integrates the lighting and design beautifully. The creamy reflective surfaces of the walls and ceiling work well to help provide a harmonious ambience. Four torchieres, one for each corner, provide a major amount of the fill light along with an illuminated step skylight detail.

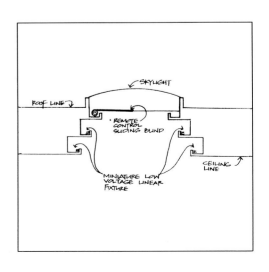

Lighting Designer
Randall Whitehead

Interior Designer
Kent Wright

Photographer
Stephen Fridge

This living room in San Francisco shows light-layering at its best. The soft ambient illumination comes from the fan-shaped wall sconces fitted with 120-volt mirror reflector bulbs. The dichroic reflector bounces ultraviolet light into the fixture then back out to create the pink-orange flame-like color. The recessed adjustable fixtures give dimension to the sculpture while punching out the art over the fireplace. Two brass pharmacy-type lamps provide reading light without drawing attention to themselves.

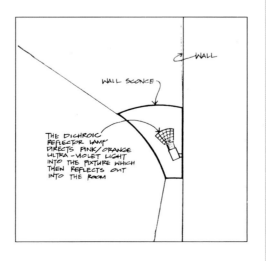

WALL

WALL SCONCE

THE DICHROIC
REFLECTOR LAMP
DIRECTS PINK/ORANGE
ULTRA-VIOLET LIGHT
INTO THE FIXTURE WHICH
THEN REFLECTS OUT
INTO THE ROOM

Lighting Designer
Randall Whitehead

Interior Designer
Kent Wright

Photographer
Stephen Fridge

The owner of this wonderful house is a true patron of the arts who constantly collects works by known and upcoming artists. These paintings and sculpture move in and out of the many rooms to the delight of guests. The recessed adjustable fixtures provide an exciting flexible accent lighting system that is as diverse as the art itself.

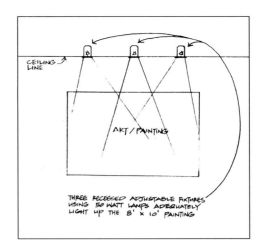

CEILING LINE

ART / PAINTING

THREE RECESSED ADJUSTABLE FIXTURES USING 50 WATT LAMPS ADEQUATELY LIGHT UP THE 8' X 10' PAINTING

Lighting Designer
Christopher Thompson

Interior Designer
Roger Newell

Photographer
David Story

This magnificent living room hovers over the city while recessed adjustable fixtures add sparkle to this stunning living space.

Lighting Designer
Christopher Thompson

Interior Designer
Roger Newell

Photographer
David Story

This ultra-lush living room makes drama the key element. A mint-green glass sculpture captures the light of a recessed adjustable fixture and shoots squiggles of refracted light onto the ceiling. Incandescent mini strip light fixtures mounted behind the stair nosing show the change in elevation to the dining area.

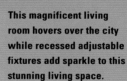

Lighting Designer
Charles J. Grebmeier and
Gunnar Burklund

Interior Designer
Charles J. Grebmeier and
Gunnar Burklund

Photographer
Eric Zepeda

To create a magical and warmly-lit environment, subtle accenting was used on artwork and sculpture without the use of downlighting.

Lighting Designer
Susan Huey

Photographer
Douglas Salin

A suspended track system adds an architectural element.

Lighting Designer
Craig Leavitt

Interior Designer
Craig Leavitt

Photographer
Russell Abraham

An ultra-modern desk is flanked by a tripod floor lamp and a pedestal with integral lighting.

Lighting Designer
Charles J. Grebmeier and
Gunnar Burklund

Interior Designer
Charles J. Grebmeier and
Gunnar Burklund

Photographer
Eric Zepeda

Self-illuminated shelves highlight the owner's extensive clock collection.

Lighting Designer
Donald Maxcy

Interior Designer
Oliver White

Photographer
Russell Abraham

Recessed adjustable fixtures highlight this wonderful collection of art objects while table lamps provide some soft light for the room.

Lighting Designer
Donald Maxcy

Interior Designer
Jan Gardner

Photographer
Russell Abraham

A slot above the fireplace throws even illumination on the painting and mantle. The slanted ceiling and glass tabletops present potential glare problems that are overcome with the precise use of recessed adjustable low-voltage fixtures.

Lighting Designer
Kenton Knapp

Interior Designer
Charles Falls and Kenton Knapp

Photographer
Eric Zepeda

Recessed down lights fitted with adaptors for sloped ceilings were used to create pools of illumination for the seating area below while recessed adjustable fixtures highlight the painting over the fireplace and art objects in the rooms. Two tabletop task lights provide an excellent shadowless reading light for the seating area.

Lighting Designer
Christopher Thompson

Interior Designer
Roger Newell

Photographer
David Story

From this angle, the living room seems to be hovering above the cityscape. The single-framed art piece has a white-lavender cast which helps draw attention to the fireplace.

Lighting Designer
Jan Moyer

Interior Designer
Donna Gleckler

Photographer
Douglas Salin

Lavender lights add a touch of fantasy to this stark, orient-inspired living room. The low-level lighting adds a feeling of intimacy as well.

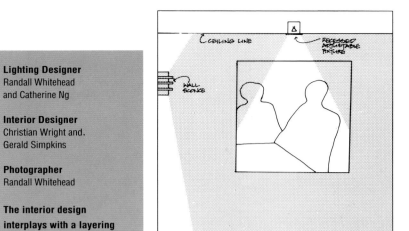

Lighting Designer
Randall Whitehead
and Catherine Ng

Interior Designer
Christian Wright and.
Gerald Simpkins

Photographer
Randall Whitehead

The interior design interplays with a layering of light sources. Recessed adjustable fixtures highlight the art and coffee table while deco-styled wall sconces produce the ambient illumination and a touch of sparkle for this living room.

Answers to Often-Asked Lighting Questions

In my work as a lighting consultant, I often see formal living rooms that look abandoned. "No one ever sits in there," the homeowner tells me. Yet, after we change the lighting, this unused room suddenly becomes the hub of the home. Family and friends gravitate to what is now a warm and inviting place.

Most homeowners are not aware that they can control light and that light affects the mood and function of every room. Lighting can create an ambiance, enhance a work area, and give the illusion of greater depth or scale. The same "psychology" of light used to sell products can be used to show off possessions, highlight art and architecture, or simply make a home brighter and more appealing.

But where do you start? The lighting industry is changing rapidly and more and more new products are appearing. The consumer can get confused. To keep up with the latest advances in design and products, many homeowners — as well as architects, interior designers, and landscapers — are turning to lighting specialists for advice on attractive, energy-efficient, low-maintenance lighting systems. The more you know about lighting, the better you can guide your consultant in creating a lighting design that is right for your home. Here are answers to the most common questions homeowners ask when choosing a lighting system.

Should I install track lighting or recessed lighting?

When track lighting was first introduced, it was considered the answer to all lighting problems. People loved the flexibility and the high-tech look. Only after the novelty wore off did those who had installed track systems begin to notice the drawbacks.

Track is best when it is used for accent lighting to highlight paintings or art objects on walls and tables. It cannot provide adequate fill light (also called ambient light), which is the light that softens and warms a room. When light from a track system falls directly on seating areas, it casts hard shadows on those below. Track lighting is also a poor choice for task lighting for the same reason — you end up working in your own shadow.

Track can work very well as accent lighting especially when there is not enough ceiling depth for recessed lighting or in rental units where cost and portability are important.

Over the past eight years, recessed lighting has greatly improved. Most manufacturers now offer recessed adjustable fixtures that use low-voltage lamps (lamp is the lighting industry's term for a light bulb) and integral transformers (see next section). These fixtures combine the flexibility of track with the clean look of a recessed system. They usually have a 358-degree radius and a 30-degree to 45-degree aiming angle, depending on the manufacturer. A wide variety of beam spreads can be produced simply by changing the lamp. Many of these fixtures are made specifically for remodeling which makes installation into existing ceilings clean and easy.

What is low voltage?

Low voltage, according to electrical code, is anything under 50 volts (normal house current operates at 110-120 volts, also known as line voltage). The most commonly used low-voltage systems are 12 volt and 6 volt. A transformer lowers line voltage to low voltage. It can be located inside the fixture (integral) or somewhere near the fixture (remote).

Low voltage can produce more light per watt than line voltage — often as much as a three-to-one ratio. Although low-voltage systems have a higher initial cost, the advantages in energy efficiency and low maintenance are considerable.

Low-voltage lamps also come in a variety of wattages and beam spreads. You can pinpoint a bowl of flowers or light a 6-foot painting. The most popular of the low-voltage lamps right now is the MR16 (multi-mirror reflector). It is the same type of lamp used in slide projectors. The small size (approximately 2 inches by 2 inches) allows manufacturers to create smaller track fixtures and recessed fixtures with tiny apertures.

How can I get both the color-quality of incandescent light and the energy-efficiency of fluorescent?

For years, the only choice in fluorescent lamps was warm-white or cool-white. The cool-white, as we all probably remember, produced a blue-green light that made people look ghoulish. The warm-white tried to copy

the color of incandescent and got as close as a pinky-orange. Today, there are over 200 colors available in fluorescent. In addition, the technology of fluorescent components has now improved to include a non-humming, full-range dimming ballast line of fixtures.

Are skylights a good idea?

Often skylights are installed to supplement or replace electric lighting during the daytime hours. Clear glass or Plexiglass skylights project a hard beam of light, shaped like the skylight opening, onto the floor. Bronze-colored skylights cast a dimmer version of the same shape. But a white opal acrylic skylight diffuses and softens the natural light producing a more gentle light that fills the space more completely. Existing clear or bronze skylights can be fitted with a white acrylic panel at or above the ceiling line to soften the light they cast.

All skylights should have ultraviolet filters to prevent the sun from rotting or bleaching natural materials. If UV filters are not available from the skylight manufacturer, they often can be found among the stock of companies that

manufacture fluorescent outdoor signs. The original fabricator of these filtering sheets of plastic is Rohm and Haas of Philadelphia. The product is called a UF3 ultraviolet filtering acrylic sheet.

If the light well is deep enough, fluorescent strip lights can be mounted between the acrylic panel and the skylight. These inexpensive strip lights can be used at night to keep the skylight from appearing as a black hole in the ceiling.

How can one avoid glare on shiny dark countertops and backsplashes from under-cabinet fixtures?

This is a common problem and one that is the toughest to solve. Mirror-like finishes reflect everything. One solution is to install a bottom facia piece that shields the fixture from the counter-top. The light reflects off the backsplash onto the work surface. The drawback is that much of the light is caught behind the trim piece and never reaches the work surface. A second solution is to install miniature recessed, adjustable low-voltage fixtures in the cabinet. Each fixture would take up the space

about equal to that of a coffee can. These fixtures should be aimed at 45 degree angles to the work surface and louvered to avoid glare.

What is the purpose of recessed incandescent downlighting and when should it not be used?

Recessed fixtures do not provide the best type of general or ambient illumination. Since no light reaches the ceiling, the upper quadrants of the room fall into darkness. This makes the room seem smaller and

creates hard shadows on faces. In California, as stated previously, all general illumination in new kitchens and baths must be fluorescent.

Where should under-cabinet fixtures be placed?

Place task lights at a level between a person's head and the work surface, mounted tight to the face of the cabinet. Have the light reflect off the backsplash and onto the countertop. Shielding should extend 1 inch deeper than the fixture itself. This produces good, shadowless task light.

least energy-efficient. Quartz supplies approximately twice the amount of light provided by household bulbs of the same wattage. Fluorescents give three to five times the amount of incandescent household bulbs of the same wattage.

What are some of the more exciting developments in lighting that can be incorporated into the design?

Neon is fine in situations where there is a good amount of ambient noise, but in quiet areas the inherent hum can be disturbing. The transformer can be remoted to reduce the noise level. Also, be careful with color selection. Intense neon colors can shift the room's color scheme. Local electrical codes should be checked before using neon. In some jurisdictions, they don't permit neon in residential spaces.

Fiber optics provide a subtle glow of light for edge details. The illumination from a fiber optics fixture is even as long as the fiber optic is looped back into the light source or illuminated from both ends. Otherwise, the lighting will be more intense at one end. This is not a bright source of light. It should serve as a decorative source only.

Backlighting glass block creates a delightful effect. Remember, you can't light glass block directly as the light simply travels through it and your light source will be visible. You must light whatever wall or surface is behind the glass block to make the block appear illuminated.

Summary

While the new lighting components can achieve spectacular effects, more attention must be paid to lighting design in new construction or remodelling projects.

Choosing the proper fixtures and switching systems is now essential to a cohesive interior environment. If bad decisions are made early in the process, the result can be a chaotic disaster in the look of a room or space (as well as costlier replacements). Conversely, creative decisions timely made will enhance the look of the interior design and architecture in ways that people would never even dream of. Lighting is a powerful tool if people know how to use it.

Where should fixtures above cabinets be placed to achieve good indirect lighting?

Mount fixtures flush with the front of the cabinets, to prevent bright spots and to be sure objects don't block the light. Add a wood block to lift the display items to the facia level so that they are not visually cut off at the bottom.

Where can fixtures be placed to light the interior of a glass door cabinet?

Fixtures can be recessed above glass shelves. If they are wooden shelves, fixtures can be mounted horizontally on each shelf; or, if the shelves can be set back slightly, the fixtures can be run vertically on the inside edges of the doors.

In high-end, high-budget jobs, do energy considerations still apply?

Whether it's a high-end or an economy project, energy costs should be carefully considered. No one wants to spend more money on energy than is necessary. Incandescent household bulbs are the

Glossary

Absorption

Refers to a measure of the amount of light absorbed by an object instead of being reflected. Dark-colored and matte surfaces are least likely to reflect light.

Accent Lighting

Lighting directed at a particular object in order to focus attention upon it.

Ambient Lighting

The soft indirect light that fills the volume of a room with illumination. It softens shadows on people's faces and creates an inviting glow in the room.

Ballast

Device that converts electrical energy used by fluorescent, mercury vapor, high pressure sodium, or metal halide lamps so the proper amount of power is provided to the lamp.

Beam Spread

The diameter of the circle of light produced by a lamp or lamp and fixture together.

Color Rendering Index

A scale used to measure how well a lamp illuminates an object's color tones as compared with the color of daylight.

Dimming Ballast

Device used for fluorescent lamps to control the light level.

Fluorescent Lamp

A very energy-efficient type of lamp that produces light through the activation of the phosphor coating on the inside surface of a glass envelope. These lamps come in many shapes, wattages, and colors.

Footcandle

A term used to measure the amount of light hitting a surface.

Glare

A source so uncomfortably bright that it becomes the focus of attention rather than what it was meant to illuminate.

High-Intensity Discharge (H.I.D.) Lamp

A category of lamp that emits light through electricity activating pressurized gas in a bulb. Mercury vapor, metal halide, and high-pressure sodium lamps are all H.I.D. lamps. It is a bright and energy-efficient light source used mainly in exterior environments.

High Pressure Sodium

H.I.D. lamp that uses sodium vapor as the light-producing element. It provides a yellow-orange light.

Incandescent Lamp

The traditional type of light bulb that produces light through electricity causing a filament to glow.

Lamp

What the lighting industry technically calls a light bulb. A glass envelope with a gas coating or filament that glows when electricity is applied.

Low-voltage Lighting

System that uses a less than 50-volt current (commonly 12-volt) instead of 120-volt, the standard household current. A transformer is used to convert the electrical power to the appropriate voltage.

Line Voltage

The 120-volt household current, generally standard in North America

Luminaire

The complete light fixture with all parts and lamps (bulbs) necessary for positioning and obtaining power supply.

Mercury Lamp

H.I.D. lamps where light emission is radiated mainly from mercury. They can be clear, phosphor-coated, or self-ballasted. They produce a bluish light.

Metal Halide Lamp

H.I.D. lamps where light comes from radiation from metal halides. It produces the whitest light of the H.I.D. sources.

Mirror Reflector (MR16, MR11)

Miniature tungsten halogen lamps with a variety of beam spreads and wattages

PAR Lamps

Lamps (bulbs) with parabolic aluminized reflectors that give exacting beam control; there are a number of beam patterns to choose from ranging from wide flood to very narrow spot. PAR lamps can be used outdoors due to their thick glass which holds up in severe weather conditions.

Task Lighting

Illumination designed for a work surface so good shadowless light is present.

Transformer

A device which can raise or lower electrical voltage generally used for low-voltage lights.

Tungsten-Halogen

A tungsten incandescent lamp (bulb) containing gas which burns hotter and brighter than standard incandescent lamps.

Directory of Lighting Designers

James Benya, IALD, P.E.
Benya Lighting Design
3491 Cascade Terrace
West Linn, OR 97068
(503)657-9157

Gunnar Burklund
Grebmeier & Associates
1298 Sacramento Street
San Francisco, CA 94108
(415)931-1088

Ross De Alessi, IALD, MIES
Ross De Alessi Lighting Design
2815 2nd Avenue
Suite 280
Seattle, WA 98121
(206)441-0870

Linda Esselstein, MIES
1495 Altschul Avenue
Menlo Park, CA 94025
(415)854-6924

Linda Ferry, IESNA, ASID (affiliate)
Architectural Illumination
P.O. Box 2690
Monterey, CA 93942
(408)649-3711

Becca Foster
Becca Foster Lighting Design
27 South Park
San Francisco, CA 94107
(415)541-0370

Charles J. Grebmeier, ASID
Grebmeier & Associates
1298 Sacramento Street
San Francisco, CA 94108
(415)931-1088

Susan Huey
Lighting Intergration Technology, Inc.
1747 Scott Street
St. Helena, CA 94574
(707)963-7813

Kenton Knapp, Allied Member ASID
Kenton Knapp Design
P.O. Box 463
Capitola, CA 95010
(408)476-7547

Craig Leavitt, ASID
Leavitt/Weaver, Inc.
451 Tully Road
Modesto, CA 95350
(209)521-5125

Claudia Librett
Design Studio Inc.
311 East 72nd Street
Penthouse C
New York, NY 10021
(212)772-0521

Donald L. Maxcy, ASID
Donald Maxcy Design Associates
The Union Icehouse
600 East Franklin Street
Monterey, CA 93940
(408)649-6582

Janet Lennox Moyer, IALD, IES, ASID
Jan Moyer Design
6225 Chelton Drive
Oakland, CA 94611
(510)482-9193

Catherine Ng, IES
Vice Principal
Light Source
1210 18th Street
San Francisco, CA 94107
(415)626-1210

Nan Rosenblatt, Allied Member ASID
Nan Rosenblatt Interior Designs
310 Townsend Street, Suite 200
San Francisco, CA 94107

Bart Smyth
Light Source
1246 18th Street
San Francisco, CA 94107
(415)626-1210

Ruth Soforenko, ASID
Ruth Soforenko Associates
137 Forest Avenue
Palo Alto, CA 94301
(415)326-5448

Christopher Thompson
Studio Lux
5228 20th Avenue NW
Seattle, WA 98107
(206)789-4020

Robert Truax
Robert Truax Lighting Design and
Consultation
360 Arguello Boulevard
San Francisco, CA 94118
(415)668-0253

Randall Whitehead, IALD
Principal
Light Source
1246 18th Street
San Francisco, CA 94107
(415)626-1210

Directory of Photographers

Russell Abraham Photography
60 Federal Street
San Francisco, CA 94107
(415)896-6400

Patrick Barta Photography
80 South Washington Street
Suite 204
Seattle, WA 98104
(206)343-7644

John Benson Photography
130 Ninth Street
San Francisco, CA 94103
(415)621-5247

Ross De Alessi, IALD, MIES
Ross De Alessi Lighting Design
2815 2nd Avenue, Suite 280
Seattle, WA 98121
(206)441-0870

Gil Edelstein Photography
4120 Matisse Avenue
Woodland Hills, CA 91364
(818)716-8909

Stephen Fridge
Fridge Photography
325 9th Street
San Francisco, CA 94103
(415)552-6754

Ben Janken Photography
48 Agnon Avenue
San Francisco, CA 94112
(415)206-1645

Cecile Keefe Photography
P.O. Box 193367
San Francisco, CA 94119
(415)647-3330

Mary Nichols
750 North Stanley Street
Los Angeles, CA 90046
(213)228-2468

Philip Pavliger Photography
9 Decatur
San Francisco, CA 94103
(415)896-6486

Kenneth Rice Photography
456 Sixty-first Street
Oakland, CA 94609
(510)652-1752

Sharon Risedorph Photography
761 Clementina Street
San Francisco, CA 94103
(415)431-5851

Douglas Salin Photography
647 Joost Avenue
San Francisco, CA 94127
(415)584-3322

Durston Saylor
14 East 4th Street
Suite 1118
New York, NY 10012
(212)228-2468

Ron Starr Photography
4104 24th Street, #358
San Francisco, CA 94114
(415)541-7732

David Story
5609 Corson Avenue South
Seattle, WA 98108
206-764-9815

John Vaughan Photography
319 Arkansas Street
San Francisco, CA 94107
(415)550-7898

Randall Whitehead, IALD
Principal
Light Source
1246 18th Street
San Francisco, CA 94107
(415)626-1210

Eric Zepeda
775 Post Street, #610
San Francisco, CA 94109
(415)775-5957